Chimpanzees

Written by Ben Hubbard

Collins

Chimpanzees inhabit forests and woodlands in Africa.

They rest at night in nests high up.

Chimpanzees have black fur, big ears and chin hair.

Chimpanzees are born with a little tail.

An infant chimpanzee clings to its mum.

Mums help infants to understand tricks and skills.

Chimpanzees have tools to hunt.
They dig for insects with sticks.

They crack nuts with rocks.

Chimpanzees have strong arms to swing across the forest.

They can stand upright or travel on hands and feet.

Chimpanzees scan for animals that might attempt to attack.

They stand and defend as a pack.

Chimpanzees

After reading

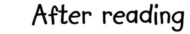

Letters and Sounds: Phase 4

Word count: 99

Focus on adjacent consonants with short vowel phonemes, e.g. /n/ /e/ /s/ /t/ /s/

Common exception words: to, the, are, they, have, little

Curriculum links (EYFS): Understanding the World

Curriculum links (National Curriculum, Year 1): Science: Animals, including humans

Early learning goals: Reading: read and understand simple sentences; use phonic knowledge to decode regular words and read them aloud accurately; read some common irregular words; demonstrate understanding when talking with others about what they have read

National Curriculum learning objectives: Reading/word reading: read accurately by blending sounds in unfamiliar words containing GPCs that have been taught; Reading/comprehension: understand both the books they can already read accurately and fluently and those they listen to by checking that the text makes sense to them as they read, and correcting inaccurate reading

Developing fluency

- Your child may enjoy hearing you read the book.
- Take turns with your child to read a page, exploring how you can use an excited tone and emphasis to stress fascinating facts.

Phonic practice

- Look at pages 7 to 8. Ask your child to find the words that begin with adjacent consonants and ask them to sound out and blend each word. (*tricks, skills*)
- Repeat for page 10. (*strong, swing*)
- If your child picks **chimpanzees** or **they**, point out how the "ch" and "th" letter pairs make only one sound (phoneme).

Extending vocabulary

- Look at pages 6 and 7. Ask your child to think of a word or phrase (synonym) that means the same as the following:
  - **infant** (e.g. *youngster, baby chimp*)
  - **clings to** (e.g. *clutches, hangs on to*)
  - **understand** (e.g. *learn, work out*)